Generational Roots

Growing in God's Goodness

Faith Hopey

Psalm 100:5 NLT

For the Lord is good. His unfailing love continues forever, and his faithfulness continues to each generation.

AKA Christian Publishing, LLC
Winder, GA 30680
470-773-8649;
info@akachristianpublishing.com

ISBN: 979-8-9936754-1-1

This book is intended to encourage, inform, and inspire readers in their walk of faith. While every effort has been made to ensure biblical accuracy and integrity, neither the author nor the publisher makes any representation or warranty as to the completeness, accuracy, or applicability of the material contained herein. Scripture references are included for study and reflection purposes only.

The author attests that all material is original or properly credited and does not infringe upon the rights of others. The responsibility for the accuracy of facts, interpretations, and opinions expressed rests solely with the author.

This publication is not intended to replace the study of God's Word, prayer, or the guidance of the Holy Spirit. Readers are encouraged to seek personal discernment and, where appropriate, pastoral counsel when applying the insights shared.

The publisher assumes no liability for any loss or damages alleged to be caused, directly or indirectly, by the information presented in this work.

To my Mammaw & Pappaw:

For all the seeds that rooted my heart in Jesus
and to all the oak treas that stand tall
because of your love.

ENDORSEMENTS

In an over opinionated world, this book is a refreshing relief. The simplicity of core values and biblical text ring louder than any hidden agenda.

Faith Hopey allows the Bible to speak for itself and guides the reader(s) to see that they are worthy of knowing who God is.

Joy Rogers
www.mapletreecfg.org

Generational Roots by Faith Hopey is a wonderful resource for Christ followers at any stage of their journey. This small, yet powerful book is truly for everyone. Each page is loaded with Scripture, yet concise and easy to read, and carries the weight of God's truth and love.

Faith writes with a grace and authority that reflects her pastoral heart and her seasoned walk with Jesus. Everyone that knows Faith knows that she authentically exudes God's love and His presence spills over onto whoever is around her. I love that she included a chapter on "Presence" and personally found that portion to be so valuable.

Faith has done a beautiful job of condensing a wealth of wisdom and revelation without compromising depth, making this book a rich guide for personal growth, discipleship, and an amazing tool for small groups.

Amber Ratliff

www.amber-leilani.com

Generational Roots lays out foundational biblical truths in a simple and comprehensive manner. The text leaves plenty of room for group dialogue and introspection amongst believers. Whether you're a long time believer walking in deep waters with Christ or just scratching the surface, *Generational Roots* will meet you where you are while furthering your understanding of God's word.

Haley Polk

www.olivebranchcattleco.com

"She has history with God." This was my very first thought when I met Faith Hopey. She had been visiting our church for the first time during a worship night. We had recently moved to a new city on the Word of the Lord, and we were greatly missing our homeschool community. It was in that community of fiery followers of Jesus that we had learned (after years and years of pastoring) what the Body of Christ could look like. Now? Now, I was looking into the eyes of a woman who had been looking at the Man with fire in His eyes, and talking with her felt like I was "home" again. I soon learned that not only was Faith a Family Pastor, but she was a true shepherd of people's hearts. As our friendship grew, I noticed many wonderful things about Faith, and here are just a few:

- She loves Jesus with her whole heart.
- She loves people (family, friends, and strangers) with her whole heart.
- In the words of a powerful line in her book: "She teaches what she knows. She imparts what she lives."

Over the past 20+ years my husband and I have had the honor and privilege of pastoring and pouring into children, teens, and adults. Discipleship, we have learned, is so necessary for those looking to walk closely with the Lord, and yet so challenging to find the proper resources that rightly convey the heart of God. The definition of discipleship is this: "The process of becoming a follower of a person or teaching, especially through intentional learning and living out those beliefs." This type of discipleship doesn't come through mentorship, but rather a nurturing mother or father who desires to see others go farther than they ever could. Faith is that momma, and this book is a gift to all who desire to be a disciple of Jesus.

Generational Roots: Growing in God's Goodness is a resource that gives leaders the tools to teach others on the very nature, character, presence, ministry, gifts and heart of God in beautiful detail. It is laid out in such a simple and organized way that is easy to understand, while also digging deep and mining the scriptures for truth. As I read this book, I couldn't help but dream of the possibilities it holds…sharing it with my family, friends, or starting a small group. Whether you are a pastor of a church, or the pastor of your home; whether you are going to dive into it for yourself or with your spouse; whether you're starting a small group or engaging in one-on-one discipleship - do not miss out on the chance to encounter the Lord through this book. I truly believe each page is Holy Spirit breathed and dripping with Heavenly wisdom that will lead you right to the heart of Jesus, the same Jesus whose reflection I saw in Faith's eyes the day I met her. Dear reader, enjoy reading this treasure, with one request…don't keep it to yourself!

Nicole Koslovsky

Co-Founder of Arrow Family Ministries
www.arrowfamily.org

Dear Reader,

The revelation of the goodness of God changed every part of my life. I remember sobbing on my kitchen floor the night I learned that He was good. It wasn't just words. I understood in the deepest depths of my heart and soul that He was FOR me. From that night on, I was never the same. With all my heart, I want you to meet this God that is better than we can even imagine.

Generational Roots will position you for deeper waters in the right current. Roots matter most to the growth of a big healthy tree. Be blessed to grow down before you grow up. These days are not for the faint of heart. You need to know what it means to be Kingdom citizens, establishing the Kingdom of God on the earth wherever you happen to be planted! Seeing God rightly will allow you to see yourself and the world rightly. Perspective is everything.

Some important facts about me and this book: I am not a theologian. I am not a Bible scholar. In fact, I'm not an expert in anything. I don't have any initials next to my name. God and I have a lot of history together. He is with me in the dark nights when there is nobody else. He gives me hope. He keeps me safe. His voice quiets the storms in my heart. He fights for my heart. Jesus is the best friend I have ever had. Through every low valley and mountain top high, His love has taught me and caught me. The Word and the presence of God ground me. He's closer than our skin, and all we need to do is become more aware of His nearness.

God isn't looking for the most qualified. He isn't looking for the most polished. He isn't looking for the best. He isn't searching the earth for the most beautiful face. God doesn't need the most talented. He's looking for the one who is most ***available***. Even if you think that you're ill-equipped and unsure how to do what He's asking of you, give Him your "Yes"!

It is our availability that changes the world.

I want this book to produce leaders who prioritize authentic relationships, point to Jesus at every turn, and inspire others to reach higher and go farther than they ever imagined.

I bless you to grow deep, tall, and wide in the revelation of the goodness of God. Christ in you is the hope this broken world is groaning for. You will spearhead restoration on the earth. You'll do it by simply falling in love with Jesus. Use this book as a resource to steward faith in your heart, in your family, in your school, at your job, in your church, and in the nations.

Warm hugs,

Faith Hopey

Instructions

This book is designed for open and slow processing in a group setting, fostering deep conversations and cultivating strong spiritual relationships — much like Jesus' interactions with the disciples. Keep it vertical AND horizontal. The Kingdom of God looks like family. Different levels of spiritual maturity, different perspectives, and different voices from all walks will accelerate and strengthen everyone's faith. Be encouraged to find healthy leaders, moms and dads in the faith, to help lead the group into deeper waters.

Here is a basic list of what a healthy leader looks like — nobody is perfect, but you want to see most of these from anyone you are learning from and with:

- They consistently have self-awareness of how they are (a sound mind).
- They have emotional intelligence (compassion, empathy, and the capacity to hold space for other people's thoughts and feelings in a safe manner).
- They are secure in their identity — not threatened by you or anyone else. They should not be fawning over others or people-pleasing at every turn.
- They are great listeners.
- They're honest. Even when you don't like what they're saying, the truth should resonate.
- They prioritize alignment over assignment — family before the work of ministry.
- They want you to stand on their shoulders. Their ceiling should be your floor. They want your revelations to be bigger than their own. They want you to believe bigger than they ever did.
- They are comfortable with being wrong or not knowing the answers. The walk in humility.

- They have strong, loving relationships both within and outside their immediate family.
- They have a life that bears fruit of the Holy Spirit.

Each lesson is one to two pages long, designed to be taught within 10 to 30 minutes, giving more time to build relationships in a group learning atmosphere. You will need a Bible anytime you open this book. This book uses the NLT translation. Several other versions I suggest are NKJV, ESV, CSB, THE PASSION, & THE AMPLIFIED.

Note: You can and will find Scriptures that seem to directly contradict some of what is written in this resource. The tension in these seemingly contradictory Scriptures actually holds revelation. Desiring approval of their personal convictions, opinions, or manmade doctrines, Christians have been known to take seemingly contradictory Scriptures and use them as weapons against other Christians. It's sword fighting with Scriptures. I wouldn't suggest learning from people who participate in weaponizing the Bible–and, please, try not to be one of them.

Use this resource to dig deeper! Find more Scriptures. Consider your own thoughts about the different topics mentioned, and then ask God every single question in your heart. You have permission to disagree. You have permission to add, subtract, and multiply!

There is a process attached to spiritual growth and maturity called sanctification. It's an everyday process, and it's not always comfortable. 1 Timothy 4:8 NLT says, "*Physical training is good, but training for godliness is much better, promising benefits in this life and in the life to come.*" A little further down, verse 10 says, "*This is why we work hard and continue to struggle, for our hope is in the living God, who is the Savior of all people and particularly of all believers.*" He is worth the discomfort.

Disclaimer

You may notice at some point that this book doesn't focus much on hell, the enemy, or the demonic realm. Because of this, many will disregard this resource as a "watered-down" gospel that focuses mostly on God. Some feel more confident in the devil's ability to deceive them than the Holy Spirit's ability to reveal all truth to them. What a bummer.

There is a spirit of religious legalism that desperately wants you focused on the enemy at all times. **The strategy of hell is fear!** Fear keeps you frozen. Fearing the enemy or the demonic realm will have you waking up in the morning with one purpose: to rebuke an enemy who has already been completely defeated. This constant gaze at the enemy is the human way to satisfy fear inside the heart. Living this way keeps us distracted from our God-given purpose.

Additionally, enemy-focused mindsets/belief systems tend to skirt around personal responsibility, blaming everything on a very powerful devil. A speeding ticket, for example, is not the work of the devil or spiritual warfare - if you were speeding. Too much focus on the enemy has the potential to create irresponsible individuals and, consequently, **a powerless church.**

I believe that knowing the heart of God is enough. By knowing Him, you'll have access to discernment, revelation, wisdom, power, and authority over fear or anything else the enemy may try to throw at you. Partnering with the heart of God in prayer and intercession is the best way to wage war over circumstances and relationships, without resorting to fear and manipulation to control outcomes or people.

Knowing how a recipe usually tastes helps you notice when it doesn't taste quite right. The more you know about God and His Kingdom, the more you'll recognize the schemes of the enemy. While training the disciples, Jesus was getting the reality of the Kingdom of God deep inside their hearts. If that's what Jesus focused on, that's what we should focus on.

While you learn from this resource, you will **not** learn to give the enemy credit, attention, power, or authority. The emphasis here will be Christ at every turn. **The goal of this book is simply that you come to have a personal, authentic relationship with the One who made you. The One who has made His home inside of you knows you best and loves you most. His name is Jesus Chri**st.

Contents

1. FOUNDATION

1.1 Three in One

1.2 The Old Covenant

1.3 The Gospel Part 1

1.4 The Gospel Part 2

1.5 The New Covenant

1.6 Water Baptism

1.7 The Bible

Lesson 1.1 | Three in One

God is ONE being in three distinct persons: God, Jesus, and the Holy Spirit. They are the beginning of everything and the end of everything.

The three-in-one God is referred to as "The Holy Trinity." These three members are coequal, co-eternal, and co-divine, and they are perfectly submitted to one another.

You and I are invited to embrace an unimaginable mystery about God. He is Holy. Holy means "different" or "separate" from anything we have ever seen or known.

How They Function Distinctly

GOD: Father / Creator / Life-Giver / Protector / Just Judge

NOTE: God's justice is quite different from the justice system we know. It's important to note that God will pursue justice in ways that look loving and kind. Not all justice is vengeful and retaliatory.

1 Corinthians 8:6

But for us, there is one God, the Father, by whom all things were created and for whom we live.

JESUS: Friend / Savior / King / High Priest / Good Shepherd / Teacher

John 3:16

For this is how God loved the world: He gave his one and only Son, so that everyone who believes in him will not perish but have eternal life.

HOLY SPIRIT: Comforter / Nurturer / Revealer / Intercessor / Advocate / Counselor / Teacher

John 14:26

But when the Father sends the Advocate as my representative — that is, the Holy Spirit — he will teach you everything and will remind you of everything I have told you.

How they function as one

The three distinct persons of the Trinity are perfectly submitted to one another and have the same motivations, goals, and heart. All three work together to win our hearts and bring us into a relationship with Him.

Song Suggestion: "Magnificent Trinity" by Melissa and Johnathan Helser

Lesson 1.2 | The Old Covenant

The Old Covenant is a term used to describe the relationship between God and Israel (His people). The Old Covenant was the law that governed that relationship.

This law was / is not possible to achieve and could never be satisfied by an imperfect human.

- The Old Covenant consists of the 10 Commandments plus 600 other moral laws. God gave these to Moses around 1400 BC (Before Christ).
- The Old Covenant emphasized works and what people must do for God.
- The 10 Commandments (Exodus 19 and 20 — *Paraphrased*)

  Don't worship any other god.

  Don't make anything or anyone into an idol.

  Don't misuse God's name or do evil in God's name.

  Don't do your usual work on the seventh day of the week – treat it as a special holy day.

  Always respect your parents.

  Don't murder anyone.

Don't commit adultery.

Don't steal from anyone.

Don't tell lies about someone else.

Don't be envious of anyone's house, their partner, or anything they own.

Galatians 3:23-24

Before the way of faith in Christ was available to us through Jesus, we were kept in protective custody. The law was our guardian until Christ came; it protected us until we could be made right with God through faith.

Consider other things that might have been true about God during this time before Jesus.

- Do you believe God is the same yesterday, today, and forever?
- What could that imply concerning the law and all the ways God is described in the Old Covenant?

Lesson 1.3 | The Gospel Part 1

The word *gospel* means: GOOD NEWS.

In the Bible, the first four books of the New Testament gives four different accounts of Jesus' life written by Matthew, Mark, Luke, and John the Beloved.

Jesus came to reveal the heart of God on earth.

John 17:25-26

O righteous Father, the world doesn't know you, but I do; and these disciples know you sent me. I have revealed you to them, and I will continue to do so. Then your love for me will be in them, and I will be in them.

Jesus proved God's love for us when He died on the cross for our sake. The gospel isn't about you accepting God. It's all about you realizing that God accepts and chooses you.

READ OUT LOUD: John 3:16

READ OUT LOUD: John 15:13

READ OUT LOUD: Romans 5:8

Salvation is MUCH more than being saved from hell!

READ OUT LOUD: Colossians 1 and Ephesians 1

Paul explains the inheritance we walk in NOW because of Christ's work and love for us.

READ OUT LOUD: Acts 2:42-47

Song Suggestion: "Simple Gospel" by United Pursuit

Lesson 1.4 | The Gospel Part 2

John 14:6

Jesus told him, "I am the way, the truth, and the life. No one can come to the Father except through Me."

Jesus the WAY:

The life of Jesus is a model for what our lives should look like. He walked out all the fruits of the Spirit: gentleness, kindness, self-control, love, joy, peace, faithfulness, & patience. His "WAY" is fruitful. His life is a model for us.

Note: Jesus also came to reveal the WAY the Father sees us.

Jesus the TRUTH:

Jesus is the door to the Father. He invites us to partake of the true divine nature of God. Where the Father had been misunderstood before, Jesus came to set the record straight.

In Matthew 5-7, Jesus gives the Sermon on the Mount, which contrasts interpretations of the Old Covenant law with the New Covenant of love.

Example: Jesus says, "*You've heard it said, but I say…*"

Note: Jesus reveals the TRUTH about what the Father believes about us.

Jesus the LIFE:

Jesus gave up His life to give us access to an "abundant" life. Scripture says the only way for us to really live in Christ is to die just as He did and to be raised up as He was, laying down our old flesh-driven lives for new Spirit-driven lives.

Note: Jesus reveals to us the abundant LIFE that the Father designed for us as He walked in perfect union with the Father. We have not been called by God to physically die. Jesus has already accomplished physical death and shed blood as the perfect sacrifice on the cross. This is one of the mysteries we embrace as believers. Practically, we lay down our **human desires** (wealth, material things, fame, sexual desires, etc.) to embrace a life in the Spirit and **new desires** birthed from a relationship with God, which produces good fruit in our lives.

The way, the truth, and the life really answers all of life's questions.

What you believe deep in your heart will drive the behaviors of your life.

The truth you believe must be wrapped up in and around Jesus. There is no gray area! No other god will do. No other god can save you. No other god can heal you. No other god can give you peace in a storm. No other god can satisfy the longing in your heart.

Jesus is the only way, the only truth, and the only life.

Song Suggestion: "Consider Him" by Abbie Gamboa, UPPEROOM

Lesson 1.5 | The New Covenant

Romans 10:4

For Christ has already accomplished the purpose for which the law was given. As a result, all who believe in him are made right with God.

The New Covenant (Jesus) has come to give us a new law of love.

God has always wanted our hearts.

READ OUT LOUD: Romans 6

You are no longer under the law, but under grace.

READ OUT LOUD: Galatians 2:15-21

The whole book of Galatians contrasts the old and new covenants and emphasizes that salvation comes through faith in Jesus Christ, not through the rules of the law!

READ OUT LOUD: Hebrews chapters 8-10

The book of Hebrews is summed up like this: I know you've known the law, but look at Jesus. He showed us a new way. Follow His way!

The Old Covenant was written before Jesus' birth. No one had a full picture of the Father until Jesus came and revealed Him. The incredible way God sovereignly still points to His precious Son Jesus all through the Old Covenant is stunning.

The New Covenant in my own words:

(Read this out loud. Write it in your heart.)

Christ is alive in me.

I can take hold of my forgiveness and believe God has made me whole.

I am tethered and partnered with God in all things.

I am fully known and fully loved.

God has given me power and authority to overcome.

I don't have to earn my way to God.

I don't have to work for His love. I can rest.

I am never alone, set aside, abandoned, or rejected.

I don't have to kill an animal to access His presence.

Nothing can separate me from God.

He can handle me on my bad days.

He's affectionate toward me.

I can be honest with Him.

When I call, He answers.

IT'S THE BEST NEWS!

Lesson 1.6 | Water Baptism

Water Baptism is not *just* a symbol.

When you agree with the transforming love of God in your life and become baptized, your obedience acts as a force of momentum for your life. It's a prophetic declaration that propels you forward in Christ.

Baptism is ***not*** what saves us. Only Jesus saves us!

Before we are baptized, we must believe that Jesus is the Son of God, that He died on the cross to pay for our sins, that He was buried, and that He resurrected and lives inside of us even now!

READ AND DISCUSS: Romans 6

Water Baptism Explained

- We are completely dunked down in the water, symbolizing burial with our Lord. We are baptized into His death on the cross and are no longer slaves to self, sin, or death.

- When we are raised out of the water, we are symbolically resurrected — raised to new life with power in the Holy Spirit.
- The blood of Jesus washes us clean when we are saved, just as water cleanses the flesh.

Water baptism OUTWARDLY illustrates the spiritual reality of the INSIDE.

1 Peter 3:21

And that water is a picture of baptism, which now saves you, not by removing dirt from your body, but as a response to God from a clean conscience. It is effective because of the resurrection of Jesus Christ.

Matthew 3:11

I baptize with water those who repent of their sins and turn to God. But someone is coming soon who is greater than I am —so much greater that I'm not worthy even to be his slave and carry his sandals. He will baptize you with the Holy Spirit and with fire.

Lesson 1.7 | The Bible

The Bible is ALIVE and ACTIVE (Hebrews 4:12).

Reading the Bible can be tricky if nobody gives you tips or tricks to help you understand it. Here are some helpful steps:

Step 1:
Open invitation to the Holy Spirit.

Anytime you open the Bible, ask the Holy Spirit to come and reveal all truth to you. Fresh revelation comes to the same old Scriptures every time you read them when the Holy Spirit breathes on them.

Step 2:
Know the original intent, culture, and context of what you are reading.

If you read the Bible without understanding the cultures, times, and languages in which it was written, you're going to misinterpret frequently. This is where you dig deeply to seek and find. Invite mentors and leaders to study with you. Find resources such as commentaries, and never forget to invite the Holy Spirit to help you understand the text. Don't read just one or two verses. Read a whole chapter or a whole book in one sitting.

Step 3:

Focus on the BIG picture until the little things come into focus.

Trust the process.

Understand the big picture! The little details will come into focus as you lean in on the big overall themes. Consider reading the whole Bible before you draw any big conclusions about God.

Step 4:

Keep an open heart.

The Pharisees memorized Scripture, but when Jesus was walking the earth as a person doing miracles, signs, and wonders, they couldn't see that He was God. They were offended by freedom. The Bible holds mysteries. Read it with an open mind and heart. Stay flexible!

Step 5:

Stay unoffended. The Bible is not a formula.

Define these words: *logos* & *rhema*

Don't take the logos word without the rhema word. Don't take the rhema word without the logos word. The two should always agree with one another. If they don't, PAUSE.

Step 6:

The Bible should lead you to a relationship with the author.

If the Bible isn't leading you to an authentic relationship, SEEK HELP!

2. TRUTH

LESSON 2.1 | The Word

<u>John 1:1-5</u>

In the beginning the Word already existed. The Word was with God, and the Word was God. He existed in the beginning with God. God created everything through him, and nothing was created except through him. The Word gave life to everything that was created, and his life brought light to everyone. The light shines in the darkness, and the darkness can never extinguish it.

Word of Life = The Holy Spirit-inspired written WORD (Bible) & Jesus in the flesh.

"...the life was made manifest" (1 John 1:2 ESV) — means that Jesus (the way, the truth, and the life) came as the Word of God wrapped in human flesh.

"...so that you too may have fellowship with us; and indeed, our fellowship is with the Father and with his Son Jesus Christ" (1 John 1:3 ESV) — means that you are invited to partake in a relationship with Jesus.

<u>Hebrews 4:12</u>

For the word of God is alive and powerful. It is sharper than the sharpest two-edged sword, cutting between soul and spirit, between joint and marrow. It exposes our innermost thoughts and desires.

2 Timothy 3:16-17

All Scripture is inspired by God and is useful to teach us what is true and to make us realize what is wrong in our lives. It corrects us when we are wrong and teaches us to do what is right. God uses it to prepare and equip his people to do every good work.

The written word of God is called the ***"logos"*** word.

The voice of God in real time or when He speaks through His word in revelation is called the ***"rhema"*** word of God.

YOU NEED BOTH!

Lesson 2.2 | No Separation

Romans 8:38-39

And I am convinced that nothing can ever separate us from God's love. Neither death nor life, neither angels nor demons, nor our fears for today nor our worries about tomorrow — not even the powers of hell can separate us from God's love. No power in the sky above or in the earth below — indeed, nothing in all creation will ever be able to separate us from the love of God, revealed through the Christ Jesus our Lord.

James 1:17

Whatever is good and perfect is a gift coming down to us from God our Father, who created all the lights in the heavens. He never changes or casts a shifting shadow.

Our God is not unstable. His love is not fragile. He is not changing His mind about us.

READ OUT LOUD: Psalm 139

Everything we do, say, think, believe — He sees it all. That can be scary to realize, but it's actually amazing. He's perfectly aware of our hang-ups, our life experiences, our shortcomings, our failures, and despite it all, He loves us more than we can imagine. He chose us and keeps choosing us!

The promise to never leave us or forsake us is one that we can hang our hat on. It's a never-moving love. As we become more aware of His presence with us all the time, we learn to receive His love in every moment.

Understand: **BELIEF DRIVES ALL OF OUR BEHAVIORS!**

When you sin or fail, do not believe the lie that God wants you to withdraw in shame!

Shame cannot live where repentance is. Turn around. Do a metaphoric U-turn! Change the thinking that drove you to bad behavior. Go to God to be renewed with right thinking for better choices down the road. He's not afraid of your bad choices. His blood is more than enough for all of it! He won't reject you. He won't abandon you. He wants your heart and your honest feelings.

Lesson 2.3 | Holy Spirit

John 15:26 27

But I will send you the Advocate — the Spirit of truth. He will come to you from the Father and will testify all about me. And you must also testify about me because you have been with me from the beginning of my ministry.

Read Outloud: John 14:17

The Holy Spirit is the great REVEALER, always revealing Jesus and the Father, and always leading us in true revelation. The Holy Spirit leads us into ALL truth.

THE HOLY SPIRIT HAS COME!

READ AND DISCUSS: ACTS 2

The Holy Spirit has made a home inside of us.

Ephesians 1:13

And now you Gentiles have also heard the truth, the Good News that God saves you. And when you believed in Christ, he identified you as his own by giving you the Holy Spirit, whom he promised long ago.

READ OUT LOUD: 1 Corinthians 6:19

1 Corinthians 2:10-11

But it was to us that God revealed these things by his Spirit. For his Spirit searches out everything and shows us God's deep secrets. No one can know a person's thoughts except that person's own spirit, and no one can know God's thoughts except God's own Spirit.

GROUP DISCUSSION:

The Holy Spirit lives IN you for you (Romans 8:9).

The Holy Spirit is UPON you for the sake of those around you (Isaiah 61).

Song Suggestion: "Holy Spirit" by Katie Torwalt

Lesson 2.4 | Power

The Holy Spirit was given to you from God so that you could have the same power Jesus had.

Discuss the power Jesus had. Look through Matthew, Mark, Luke, and John to discover Jesus and His life that is now our inheritance.

This power is not for the purpose of gaining control over other people or obtaining influence and money.

Power from God makes our lives **fruitful**.

You have the power to have qualities that make you attractive to the world. **This is how you light up the dark!**

READ OUT LOUD: Acts 2:17-21

READ OUT LOUD: Galatians 5:22-23

We need the Holy Spirit's power for UNLIMITED love, joy, peace, patience, kindness, goodness, faithfulness, gentleness, and self-control.

<u>Acts 1:8</u>

But you will receive power when the Holy Spirit comes on you, and you will be my witnesses in Jerusalem, and in all Judea and Samaria, and to the ends of the earth.

2 MAIN REASONS WE NEED FRUITFUL LIVES:

- We benefit a great deal!
- Our lives point others to Jesus. The fragrance of our fruit attracts people to Him!

A fruitful life is what it looks like to walk out our true identity, which has already been established. We don't work FOR our identity in Christ to earn anything. We live FROM confidence in who we are, experiencing the love of God in and through us.

God created us strategically. We are hard-wired and designed for power. His power flows through us. We have aid in all situations. Without Him, we are powerless to be fruitful.

Lesson 2.5 | Freedom

John 8:31-32

Jesus said to the people who believed in him, "You are truly my disciples if you remain faithful to my teachings. And you will know the truth, and the truth will set you free."

Believing Jesus is the truth sets you free. He is the way, the truth, and the life!

FREE FROM WHAT?

Free from sin, death, lies from the enemy, depression, all kinds of addiction, fear, bitterness, control, torment, anxiety… and the list goes on and on!

Most of the time, deliverance that leads to freedom is a process. You become a new creation, making one tiny decision at a time over a long period of time. In this process, God grows your character and strengthens your faith so you can see that nothing in your life has been wasted.

NOTE: We are ALL being transformed by the renewing of our minds. Not one person is exempt from the hard part of denying our flesh to be in communion with Christ.

Accountability can help. Find someone you trust to love you through the good, the bad, and the ugly. BE HONEST with that person.

Romans 12:2

Don't copy the behavior and customs of this world, but let God transform you into a new person by changing the way you think. Then you will learn to know God's will for you, which is good and pleasing and perfect.

God wants us to be powerful, so He gave us the Holy Spirit! We are designed to overcome sin. We are designed to overcome the schemes of the enemy. We are designed to build layers of faith inside of us (brick by brick) that strengthen us for the days we live in and the temptations that present themselves.

You steward your own freedom. Stand firm. Make hard decisions every day. It won't feel like striving if you are falling in love with Jesus. **Get hungry**, and let Him fill you up with His love.

Connection to God is where freedom is found. Stay plugged in. It won't be perfect every day. Build history and a testimony with God. He already sent HELP for us for when it's hard. But we have to be responsible and humble enough to lean in and ask for help!

3. NATURE & CHARACTER

3.1 God is Love

3.2 Taste & See

3.3 Nature Reveals God

3.4 Sovereignty

Note: The main thing you need to take away from this section is that God's character and nature are defined through the life of Jesus, who came to reveal the true heart of God. Jesus' life is on display to reveal the Father, and it's all written in the gospels — Matthew, Mark, Luke, & John.

Lesson 3.1 | God is Love

<u>1 John 4:16 NLT</u>

We know how much God loves us, and we have put our trust in his love. God is love, and all who live in love live in God, and God lives in them.

God doesn't just love you. **He IS love.**

No matter what, He will always love you. Love is His nature. Love is His response to everything. Love is His position. Love is His communication style. Jesus proved God's love for you on the cross.

He loves us UNIQUELY. Parents often discuss how they didn't know if there would be enough love in their hearts for the second or third child. But the heart expands, and we love our children according to their uniqueness. I don't love my daughter the same way I love my son. It's not a lesser love. It's a unique love. If I had two daughters, I would love each of them for who they are. This is how God loves us. You are irreplaceable. There is space in His heart that is reserved only for you!

God's love is unlimited. God's love is called "Perfect Love," which means "Mature Love" — it's the best love. God's love is forever! It never gives up. Never fails. Never stops. It's not like any other love you have ever known.

READ OUT LOUD: Psalm 136

His faithful love endures forever!

READ OUT LOUD: 1 John 4:9-16

READ OUT LOUD: Romans 8:37-39

You can read about God's love and memorize every Scripture about it, but still not really know His love for you. Try to remember a time when you felt loved by God. Maybe He answered a prayer, or you felt His presence during worship. His presence is the best place to encounter His love. Stay plugged in!

Leaders: Share your favorite Scriptures or chapters on the love of God.

Spend time in His presence. Pause. Write down what you hear and how you feel. Experience and encounter His love for you.

Lesson 3.2 | Taste & See

What you need: Strawberries & Blueberries.

Let's define ***"nature"*** and ***"character."***

***Nature*:** The basic or inherent features of something.

The nature of a wild bear is very different from the nature of a trained dog. Using this example, you could even talk about the word "instinct." In people, we can see their true nature through their "knee-jerk" reaction--how they respond before they have time to even think..

***Character*:** The distinctive qualities of an individual.

What are the characteristics of a strawberry versus a blueberry? How can you tell them apart by looking at and tasting them? What comes to mind about a particular person the moment their name is mentioned?

How do we come to know God's ***nature*** and ***character***?

How do we know what He looks like, sounds like, feels like?

Psalm 34:8

Taste and see that the LORD is good. Oh, the joys of those who take refuge in him!

Tasting has to do with experiencing. Seeing has to do with perspective.

We know His nature and character by reading and learning about Jesus, experiencing His presence, and encountering His love.

GROUP DISCUSSION: Take turns **wondering** about the nature and character of God. Take plenty of time for this.

By growing in the revelation of His goodness, you will see God rightly, see yourself rightly, and see the world rightly.

READ IT OUT LOUD: Psalm 104

John 1:5

The light shines in the darkness, and the darkness can never extinguish it.

Romans 8:28

And we know that God causes everything to work together for the good of those who love God and are called according to his purpose for them.

Lesson 3.3 | Nature Reveals God

<u>Romans 1:20</u>

Forever, since the world was created, people have seen the earth and sky. Through everything God made, they can clearly see his invisible qualities — his eternal power and divine nature.

Think about outer space. Think about the vast ocean.

Scientists haven't yet discovered all the galaxies in space. It just keeps going! They don't know the deepest depths of the ocean yet. They can't find the end.

God is like that! Creation reveals God. He is the creator of all things.

When you create art (music, drawing, painting, dancing), it reflects who **you** are. Art that you create expresses your perspective and your nature. The same is true for God.

Think about a green and lush meadow. Imagine a place that puts peace in your heart just by beholding it. **God is like that.**

Imagine a raging waterfall expressing strength in the middle of nowhere. **God is like that.**

You may wonder, "What about a hurricane or a tornado? What about the destructive parts of nature? Do they represent God's nature, too?"

QUESTIONS ARE GOOD!

QUESTIONS LEAD YOU TO TRUTH!

STAY WITH JESUS!

Because there are Old Testament and New Testament stories that explain that God authored destruction, some would say God causes destruction.

Some believe that ever since the fall in Genesis, man has been returning to the revelation of the goodness of God. What was written was from the perspective that the writers had at the time, before Jesus came to reveal who God really is.

Keep in mind, you were made in His image. It is my opinion that whatever you believe is true about God is what you will believe is true about you. What we believe about His nature matters a great deal.

You'll need to dig into the word to find your own heart posture on this. Invite the Holy Spirit to reveal all truth to you. Ask plenty of questions. It's okay not to know everything. Some revelations take time to develop.

Lesson 3.4 | Sovereignty

People tend to blame God for bad things that happen. From the death of a loved one, to a speeding ticket, to a toothache, to bankruptcy… The list goes on and on.

<u>John 16:33</u>

Here on earth, you will have many trials and sorrows. But take heart, because I have overcome the world.

Bad things in our lives happen for three reasons:

1. **The enemy:** Satan comes as a thief to steal, kill, and destroy (John 10:10).
2. **Our choices:** We make choices, and there are consequences for EVERY choice we make — good and bad. This is all through the Bible.
3. **Broken people:** Unforgiveness, unresolved trauma, and pain cause people to hurt others.

READ OUT LOUD: Romans 6:23

READ OUT LOUD: Colossians 3:25

What's so great about having a GOOD God is that, no matter the reasons why, God uses bad things for our good if we let Him. He doesn't waste hard things in our lives. He gives us beauty for ashes. He turns our sorrow to joy! **This is the Sovereignty of God.**

Isaiah 61:3

To all those who mourn in Israel, he will give a crown of beauty for ashes, a joyous blessing instead of mourning, festive praise instead of despair.

GROUP DISCUSSION:

What does this promise mean for us?

What are some truths to lean on when God doesn't seem good.

- Rejoice in the promises of God.
- Laugh at lies. (Laughing at lies disarms the lie and the liar!)
- Believe the truth more than you believe your feelings.
- Trust God - He sees the bigger picture.
- Stay tender-hearted, forgiving yourself and others often.

Song Suggestion: "Highs and Lows" by Abbie Gamboa, UPPEROOM

Lesson 4.1 | Sons & Daughters

Galatians 4:7

Now you are no longer a slave but God's own child. And since you are his child, God has made you his heir.

We have a NEW identity through Jesus.

2 Corinthians 5:17

This means that anyone who belongs to Christ has become a new person. The old life is gone; a new life has begun!

In order to represent Jesus and heaven on the earth, we MUST see ourselves the way God sees us.

We are His children. We are His friends.

John 15:15

I no longer call you slaves, because a master doesn't confide in his slaves. Now you are my friends, since I have told you everything the Father told me.

God shares secrets with His friends.

A servant only does what he has to do. Whatever he's told. Friends partner together to accomplish a common vision. As friends of God, we partner with Him to release His kingdom on the earth.

Romans 8:16-17

Don't you realize that you become the slave of whatever you choose to obey? You can be a slave to sin, which leads to death, or you can choose to obey God, which leads to righteous living. Thank God! Once you were slaves of sin, but now you wholeheartedly obey this teaching we have given you.

What is a ***coheir***? Whatever Jesus inherits, we also inherit as His ***coheir***.

What did Jesus inherit from the Father? Peace, joy, hope, a sound mind, power, self-control, gentleness, love, kindness... and God Himself! There is SO MUCH MORE.

Lesson 4.2 | Chosen

<u>1 Peter 2:9</u>

But you are not like that, for you are a chosen people. You are royal priests, a holy nation, God's very own possession. As a result, you can show others the goodness of God, for he called you out of the darkness into his wonderful light.

The word "chosen" articulates your value.
You didn't ask to be chosen. You didn't have to do anything special to be chosen.

<u>John 15:16</u>

You didn't choose me. I chose you. I appointed you to go and produce lasting fruit, so that the Father will give you whatever you ask for, using my name.

God has loved you from the beginning!

He chose you before you were made.

God has chosen you.

You have a choice to love Him or not.

Love isn't love if there's a demand for it.

Love is a choice.

We love him because He loved us FIRST.

Lesson 4.3 | Co-laborers

We are co-laborers with Christ.

WHY WAS JESUS SENT?

To reveal to us the heart of the Father and to destroy the works of the enemy.

We are called to do all the things Jesus did.

John 20:21

Again he said, "Peace be with you. As the Father has sent me, so I am sending you."

READ OUT LOUD & DISCUSS: Isaiah 61

Acts 10:38

And you know that God anointed Jesus of Nazareth with the Holy Spirit and with power. Then Jesus went around doing good and healing all who were oppressed by the devil, for God was with him.

As Christians, we are anointed like Jesus through the Holy Spirit.

Colossians 1:27

For God wanted them to know that the riches and glory of Christ are for you Gentiles, too. And this is the secret: Christ lives in you. This gives you assurance of sharing his glory.

Christ IN you means that nobody can bring the glory of God to earth like you can. Nobody can compare. There is a unique way you bring the love of Christ to the earth. If Christ lives in you, all you have to do to change the world is to BE WHO GOD HAS MADE YOU TO BE!

Song Suggestion: “Lace Up Your Boots” by Circuit Riders

Lesson 4.4 | Access & Authority

As God's children, we obtain ACCESS and AUTHORITY.

ACCESS

Hebrews 4:16

So let us come boldly to the throne of our gracious God. There we will receive his mercy, and we will find grace to help us when we need it most.

Sons & daughters have access to their Father's resources and authority to take those resources freely.

Good fathers always want to bless their kids with whatever they need. They're good at providing. God is a REALLY good Father. He's always providing what we need, and sometimes even more than we need.

AUTHORITY

Matthew 10:1

Jesus called his twelve disciples together and gave them authority to cast out evil spirits and to heal every kind of disease and illness.

Sons & Daughters have the authority to conduct business for their Father in heaven.

In Jewish culture, once a son or daughter is old enough, they usually take over the family business for their mom and dad. Jewish parents would take their children to the city gate and tell everyone that their child would be in charge of the family business moving forward. Father God has taken you to the city gate and is pointing to you! You have the authority to do business for God!

<u>He wants us armed with power and authority and operating in LOVE.</u>

What kind of business does God do?

Hint: Jesus showed us! He loved people by healing sickness, healing minds, restoring, redeeming, and taking old things and making them new!

So what kind of business do YOU have authority to do?

Lesson 4.5 | Purpose

You were made for a specific purpose!

<u>Jeremiah 29:11</u>

"For I know the plans I have for you," says the Lord. "They are plans for good and not for disaster, to give you a future and a hope."

Search for a definition of the word ***"destiny."***

We find true fulfillment when we are running in the unique destiny God has given specifically to each one of us.

<u>2 Thessalonians 1:11</u>

So we keep on praying for you, asking our God to enable you to live a life worthy of his call. May he give you the power to accomplish all the good things your faith prompts you to do.

As we mature in the Lord, desires in our hearts help reveal our specific *destiny*.

- What are some of your desires?
- What problems do you want to solve in the world?

- What brings you joy?
- What kind of people are your favorite?
- Do you know what your specific destiny is?

Our BIG PICTURE *destiny* is to represent Christ on the earth. To offer Kingdom solutions to earthly problems is our mandate.

2 Corinthians 5:20

So we are Christ's ambassadors; God is making his appeal through us. We speak for Christ when we plead, "Come back to God!"

John 20:21 NLT

Again he said, "Peace be with you. As the Father has sent me, so I am sending you."

Jesus shares His mission with us to bring heaven to earth!

Matthew 28:19-20

Therefore, go and make disciples of all the nations, baptizing them in the name of the Father and the Son and the Holy Spirit. Teach these new disciples to obey all the commands I have given you. And be sure of this: I am with you always, even to the end of the age.

Before you operate in any purpose, it's important to know that your role as a son or daughter of God is the most important purpose. Everything you DO needs to flow from your identity.

Lesson 5.1 | Joy

Joy is one-third of the Kingdom!

<u>Romans 14:17-18</u>

The kingdom of God is not a matter of what we eat or drink, but of living a life of goodness, peace, and joy in the Holy Spirit. If you serve Christ with this attitude, you will please God, and others will approve of you, too.

READ OUT LOUD: Isaiah 61

The *"oil of gladness"* and *"everlasting joy"* are prophesied as promises from God. Jesus is the fulfillment of these promises!

<u>Luke 1:44 (Paraphrased)</u>

John leapt for joy in Elizabeth's womb when he encountered Jesus in Mary's womb.

When you encounter Jesus, you encounter joy!

Nehemiah 8:10

And Nehemiah continued, "Go and celebrate with a feast of rich foods and sweet drinks and share gifts of food with people who have nothing prepared. This is a sacred day before our Lord. Don't be dejected and sad, for the joy of the Lord is your strength!"

Joy builds strength. Joy is a **WEAPON**! Joy releases kingdom empowerment.

Acts 13:52

And the believers were filled with joy and with the Holy Spirit.

Circumstances of life are happening continually.

This particular lesson is not to encourage us to laugh at life with a numb or cynical attitude.

Authentic joy is a reality that lives deeper than surface-level happiness, which is based on our circumstances. Authentic joy comes when you realize that your reality (no matter what is happening in your world) is the life and victory of Jesus.

NOTE: Many don't see how you can hold joy in seasons of grief or sorrow. Look at the Psalms. In one sentence, David is stricken with sorrow and completely defeated. Yet, in many cases, by the very next sentence, he is experiencing the peace of God, which releases joy that satisfies his soul.

Authentic joy is grace that empowers us for living boldly in the midst of hard circumstances.

Song Suggestion: "Down in My Heart" by Mountain People Worship & Suzy Yaraei

Lesson 5.2 | Cultivate

EVERYTHING in God's Kingdom is cultivated.

Definition of *cultivate*: to prepare or develop

WHAT DOES A PLANT NEED TO LIVE?

SOIL - SUN - WATER

When we plant a seed, we provide it with all the necessary elements so that it will develop and grow into a healthy, thriving plant.

Our Christian life needs certain elements to thrive, just like plants.

When we *cultivate*, we are consistently providing whatever is needed in order for things to develop and grow properly.

What elements are needed to grow and develop a friendship with our Creator?

SOME WAYS TO GROW IN THE LORD:

Worshipping — He is worthy of our praise and our worship.

Worship is not simply singing songs. Worship is how we live. Our lives poured out to honor God is really what worship is. Our small, mundane moments and our huge life-changing moments. It's all worship.

Praying — exchanging thoughts and feelings with each other.

Reading the Bible — Helps you to get to know Him. (Read the Gospels)

Quality Time — The secret place (being alone with God) cultivates love between the two of you. Love lingers.

Cultivate the presence of God in your life.

Stay aware that He doesn't live in the sky. He lives in your heart. He's closer than your breath.

Acknowledge His presence.

READ OUT LOUD & DISCUSS: Matthew 13:31-32

Lesson 5.3 | The Secret Place

<u>Matthew 6:5-6 NLT</u>

When you pray, don't be like the hypocrites who love to pray publicly on street corners and in the synagogues where everyone can see them. I tell you the truth, that is all the reward they will ever get. But when you pray, go away by yourself, shut the door behind you, and pray to your Father in private. Then your Father, who sees everything, will reward you.

READ OUT LOUD: Psalm 91

Review all the promises that come to those who stay in the secret place.

What is the secret place? A life of continual fellowship with God, who has made YOU His resting place.

Where is the secret place? In your heart.

This secret place is not something you necessarily need to keep hidden. It's okay if other people know that you have time alone with God. Secret times are special — the way best friends share secrets. God likes that time with us.

Time alone with God: A way to *cultivate* a deep relationship with God.

ACTIVATION

Spend a few minutes in a secret place right now. Go into your own space in your heart. You can go to this place no matter where you are, no matter what you are doing, no matter who is around. Practice silence. Meditate on His goodness. Talk to God from your heart. He hears even when you don't speak.

Rest is a huge part of being with God!

The enemy would LOVE for you to work really hard to be with God, burn out, and give up. Have you ever felt pressure to be a certain way with certain people in your life? With God, you get to rest. He delights in you! You don't have to work for His love. You don't have to wear any masks for God. Learn how to rest in His presence. You don't have to say anything. You don't have to do anything.

You can sit, lie, stand, sleep, sing, write, or just breathe, and it's all enough in His presence.

Song Suggestion: "House on a Hill" by Amanda Cook

Lesson 5.4 | Prayer

TALK TO GOD!

It doesn't have to be pretty or eloquent. It doesn't have to be formal. Just share your life with Him the same way you would a close friend. Honestly and authentically, say all your words.

Jesus teaches His friends how to pray.

<u>Matthew 6:9-13</u>

Our Father in heaven, may your name be kept holy. May your Kingdom come soon. May your will be done on earth, as it is in heaven. Give us today the food we need, and forgive us our sins, as we have forgiven those who sin against us.

And don't let us yield to temptation, but rescue us from the evil one.

- START WITH THANKFULNESS — Psalm 66
- SINCERE PRAYER — Matthew 6:6-8
- PRAYER IN HUMILITY — Philippians 4:6-7
- PRAY WITH CONFIDENCE — Hebrews 4:16
- PRAY WITHOUT CEASING — 1 Thessalonians 5:17
- PRAY IN THE SPIRIT — Ephesians 6:18

THERE ARE MANY MORE SCRIPTURES ON PRAYER! DIG IN!

Part of prayer is also **LISTENING** because….**GOD TALKS BACK!**

Hearing His voice isn't hard!

You were DESIGNED to hear Him. He speaks to you in your language. He speaks in your heart or in your head, and it might sound like your own voice. Pay attention to how you feel when you hear Him. His voice brings hope, peace, and joy. Even if it isn't what you want to hear, it will still come with peace. He gives instructions for your life. You need to practice hearing Him!

Other voices cause confusion, chaos, destruction, and fear. Those aren't Jesus!

A house of prayer (a church) or a PERSON of prayer will be marked by His presence.

Isaiah 56:7

"I will bring them to my holy mountain of Jerusalem and will fill them with joy in my house of prayer. I will accept their burnt offerings and sacrifices, because my Temple will be called a house of prayer for all nations."

The two go hand in hand—**Prayer & Presence.**

Don't overthink it!

Pray when you do ANYTHING and EVERYTHING!

Song Suggestion: "Our Father" by Bethel Music, Jenn Johnson

Lesson 5.5 | Hearing the Voice of God

John 10:27

My sheep listen to my voice; and I know them, and they follow me.

God made us for fellowship. He wants to communicate with us. The Father designed us to hear His voice. In Scripture, God speaks directions, instructions, destiny, expresses affection, and brings words of correction. In sharing some of the ways God speaks to us, don't box yourself in. He may speak to you in a way that is not mentioned here. That's great too! Find someone that hears like you do so you can be affirmed and sharpened.

Just like we have senses to help us receive information about the world around us, there are some practical and special ways we hear information from God.

KNOWING	knows in their gut or head
FEELING	feels the heart or emotions of God
SEEING	often has dreams at night and sees the heavenly realm in everyday life
HEARING	experiences audible voice of God

Can you see yourself in any of these four? You may hear in more than one way.

THE BIG QUESTION: You may be asking yourself, "How do I know it's God and not my own head or heart when I hear something?" Great question!

The answer is multifaceted.

First, whatever God speaks will always match up with His character and nature. We know His character and nature by looking at the life of Jesus. The bible is a great filter for what you hear. For example: God would never tell you to hate your neighbor. That contradicts the greatest commandment in the word of God.

Second, what God says to you will always be coupled with peace, joy, and hope. If what you hear causes confusion or chaos… that's not God.

Third, God often confirms His word to us. Confirmation is a funny thing because it could come in many ways that I can't begin to list. Confirmation looks different based on the nature of what God is communicating to you and how you receive information.

Fourth, practice makes perfect. Take risks. When you think you hear something from God, share it with a trusted friend to get their thoughts. Receiving honest feedback is how we grow and learn.

The number one way we hear from God is giving Him space to talk to us. Give God permission to interrupt your life with His voice. Also, find time to build a rhythm in your life of intentional listening. Not reading your bible or devotional. Not praying. Just listening.

READ OUT LOUD: 1 Kings 19:11-13

Song Suggestion: "The Voice of God" by Dante Bowe

Lesson 5.6 | Communion

Communion could be a whole book by itself. Take your time in reading these Scriptures. Get all you can out of them before moving on. We are made for communion. *Plan to take communion when you are done with this lesson.*

READ OUT LOUD: Psalm 16

We take communion to remember that the victory of Jesus is also ours. Our victory is not just defined as battles won. It includes that, but it's so much more. It's about having a victorious mindset in every part of our lives.

Communion is exchanging His strength for your weakness at every turn. It's letting His love cover our guilt and shame. It's coming into right belief about how present God really is. It's knowing the reality of your freedom and your identity in Christ.

READ OUT LOUD: Matthew 26:17-30

"Eat my flesh and drink my blood" (John 6:53-56). Most of us today would find these words offensive and wonder how we became swept up in a cult! Jesus didn't even take the time to explain these words He said. Some people ran. Who could blame them? But some people were curious enough to stay. They chose to sit in the tension of loving Jesus without fully understanding everything He said. I believe we were designed for this <u>specific</u> tension. God says something so

crazy that it doesn't make any sense, and we get the privilege of waiting for His faithfulness to reveal all truth to us.

I believe when Jesus said, "*Eat of my flesh and drink of my blood,*" He meant: "Partake of me. Take all of Me inside all of you. Take My life and put it inside of your life! Accept the invitation to share with Me in My suffering and in My victory."

READ OUT LOUD: Psalm 22

Other Suggested Scriptures:

- John 6:53-58
- Isaiah 53
- 1 Corinthians 11:17-33
- 1 John 1:1-4
- Acts 2:42

Song Suggestion: "No Life Apart" by Abbie Gamboa, UPPERROOM

Lesson 5.7 | Burning

Burning is a term we use to describe the state of our heart when it's directly affected by the priority and cultivation of the presence of God in our lives. Our hearts burn with passion for Christ.

READ OUT LOUD: Luke 24:13-34

Passion for Christ is what keeps our hearts burning for Him.

Passion is expressed through hunger and thirst.

Return to Luke 24:13-34 and highlight *hunger* and *thirst* in this story from Luke. Find where the disciples wanted more.

When our physical bodies are hungry, we eat a meal, feel full, and stop eating. In the Spirit, when we are hungry for God, we eat a meal (worship and / or the Word) and feel ravenous for more!

Burning with passion for Christ makes you a lighthouse for the world. You are a light in the dark. The world is attracted to the light in you that is Christ.

In the Psalms, David is an example of someone who burned for the Lord. No matter what his day was like, he was leaning into the Lord. He was singing, crying, and loving God through every mountain high and valley low.

Lesson 5.8 | Creativity

The Bible begins with God CREATING!

READ OUT LOUD - Genesis 1

God gives us permission to create in partnership with Him! David was, in my opinion, the most brilliant, creative person in the Bible. The book of Psalms is a work of creative genius!

Creativity in the presence of God allows us to glorify the wonder of God.

There aren't many guardrails for creativity as long as sin isn't involved.

You've been designed with imagination. Your imagination is <u>FROM</u> God and <u>FOR</u> God.

EXAMPLES OF HOW YOU CAN CREATE IN HIS PRESENCE:

Dancing	Songwriting	Fashion Design
Painting	Rythms	Graphic Design
Drawing	Flags	Woodwork

The list goes on and on. How do you create? Fill in the empty spaces in the chart with more ways to create.

Exodus 35:31-32

The Lord has filled Bezalel with the Spirit of God, giving him great wisdom, ability, and expertise in all kinds of crafts. He is a master craftsman, an expert in working with gold, silver, and bronze. He is skilled in engraving and mounting gemstones and in carving wood. He is a master at every craft. And the Lord has given both him and Oholiab, son of Ahisamach, of the tribe of Dan, the ability to teach their skills to others. The Lord has given them special skills as engravers, designers, embroiderers in blue, purple, and scarlet thread on fine linen cloth, and weavers. They excel as craftsmen and as designers.

Anything you do creatively in the presence of God is done to glorify Him! Be challenged to grow your skills and become excellent in your craft — **not for people, but for God.**

6. PASSION

6.1 Hunger & Thirst

6.2 Intimacy with God

6.3 Repentance & Revival

6.4 Nature

Lesson 6.1 | Hunger & Thirst

Passion is expressed through hunger and thirst. Passionate people always want more. People who are passionate about reading want to read all the time. They want to explore different kinds of books, as well as authors and libraries. NBA basketball players, amazing mothers, world-class chefs, YouTube influencers, or excellent personal shoppers at Walmart – they are all hungry to go after growth, knowledge, skill, and excellence. The same is true of Christians. When you are passionate about God, you want more of Him, and you seek out ways to discover more!

Psalm 42:1

As the deer longs for streams of water, so I long for you, O God.

Matthew 5:6

God blesses those who hunger and thirst for justice, for they will be satisfied.

Psalm 107:9

For he satisfies the thirsty and fills the hungry with good things.

John 6:27-29

But don't be so concerned about perishable things like food. Spend your energy seeking the eternal life that the Son of Man can give you. For God the Father has given me the seal of his approval." They replied, "We want to perform God's works, too. What should we do?" Jesus told them, "This is the only work God wants from you: Believe in the one he has sent."

John 6:35

Jesus replied, "I am the bread of life. Whoever comes to me will never be hungry again. Whoever believes in me will never be thirsty."

Hunger & thirst **ATTRACT** heaven!

These are promises from God to fill you and satisfy you when you pursue His heart.

In the NATURAL, we get full by eating a meal. In the SPIRIT, we get hungrier by eating!

HOW DO WE EAT AND DRINK GOD? by spending time with Him

- Worship (singing, dancing, shouting, devotion, quality time)
- Prayer
- Reading the Bible
- Being thankful
- Stewarding what He has given us

There is no formula for this. It's all about a heart posture that wants more of Jesus. You can want more of God driving down the road. You can want more of God while you work. You can want more of God when you do the dishes or fold laundry. This is what it looks like to really burn with passion. It's not about doing. It's about believing there is always more available and personally pursuing the more.

Lesson 6.2 | Intimacy with God

Intimacy is the result of passion. You want to be close to God, and you get to KNOW Him in the process of being close.

Note: Proximity doesn't equal a surrendered heart. You cannot have intimacy with God without surrender. A surrendered heart comes from knowing the heart of God is good and is for you. Surrender means that you love and trust God with your heart and your life. True proximity makes Him irresistible. You won't have to wonder if you can trust Him. When you see Him, you'll know you can. Proximity to Him swallows up our fear.

Philippians 3:10-11

I want to know Christ and experience the mighty power that raised him from the dead. I want to suffer with him, sharing in his death, so that one way or another I will experience the resurrection from the dead!

John 15:5

Yes, I am the vine; you are the branches. Those who remain in me, and I in them, will produce much fruit. For apart from me you can do nothing.

Luke 12:6-7

What is the price of five sparrows — two copper coins? Yet God does not forget a single one of them. And the very hairs on your head are all numbered. So don't be afraid; you are more valuable to God than a whole flock of sparrows.

READ OUT LOUD: Mark 12:41-44 & Matthew 14:18-21

Pray when you don't want to. Share with God honestly about your life. There is nothing hidden.

WAIT AND LISTEN for Him to talk back.

You won't always feel like praying. You won't always want to worship or wait to hear Him. To be mature in the Lord, you have to lay down your feelings and commune with Him daily. Not as a religious duty, but out of passion to know Him and see Him. Don't do this for what He can do for you. Do this from a heart that wants to discover more of His goodness. It never ends!

This is a huge subject with **so many** Scriptures and stories that are not listed here.

DIG IN ON YOUR OWN OR WITH YOUR GROUP!

Lesson 6.3 | Repentance & Revival

Intimacy produces repentance.

Repentance leads us to individual revival.

2 Chronicles 7:14

Then if my people who are called by my name will humble themselves and pray and seek my face and turn from their wicked ways, I will hear from heaven and will forgive their sins and restore their land.

This Scripture is not for the world full of sinners. It's actually for God's people!

I have a personal relationship with God. He lives in my heart, and I am not a slave to sin. However, pride in my heart pops up from time to time. Both are true! I am saved, and I have a pride problem sometimes. When I recognize my pride, I need to change my thinking. This is repentance. The best prayer you could ever pray is, "Help me!" I don't repent and change my thinking in my own strength. I invite God into this process and let Him change me from the inside out.

You are powerful, accountable, and responsible. Take hold of your godliness and train yourself in the Lord. You need the Holy Spirit for this work!

God gives SO MUCH grace that empowers you for a life of godliness.

READ OUT LOUD: 2 Peter 1:3 & Titus 2:11-12

Let regret teach you! Resist guilt and shame! Repent and actually change the way you think.

Remember: Your beliefs drive your behaviors.

Repentance is an invitation to think rightly.

Repentance is how God rights all the wrongs in our lives!

We choose to trust His way. He renews our minds to choose the mind of Christ, which is promised to us. When we align our minds with Christ's, we invite transformation into our lives. We receive His thoughts, His perspective, and His understanding.

READ OUT LOUD: Romans 12:2 & 1 Corinthians 2:16

Revival happens when dead things come to life and when we are set on fire from the inside out. It all starts with right thinking! God isn't looking for the right behavior.

God is looking for right thinking which births right behavior.

He cares deeply about what and who you believe!

It's the start to a lifestyle of true revival!

Lesson 6.4 | Nature

READ OUT LOUD: Ephesians 4:1-5

This Scripture explains that we are called to stretch ourselves in order to be Christlike in relationship with other believers.

Passion needs to be walked out after we have surrendered it to the Lord. Unsurrendered passion can hurt people.

Actions speak louder than words. Your nature reveals itself in your body language, the tone of your voice, and your facial expressions. When passion rises, it's important to be aware of how other people are experiencing you. It's right to be passionate. Keep in mind, you represent Christ. Your words and your actions should inspire passion in others. If your nature is a bit off, the message of what you're passionate about won't be received as well — nature should trump passion.

Passion alone cuts off ears (Peter in the garden of Gethsemane in John 18). Jesus said, t*his isn't the way*!

READ OUT LOUD: Ephesians 4:17-32

We have inherited the nature of God!

Love people where they are and call them higher with kindness and gentleness.

You can say the truth in love. <u>If it's not said in love, it's not God's nature</u>.

7. THE CHURCH

Lesson 7.1 | The Body of Christ

The body of Christ, also known as the bride of Christ, consists of individuals all over the globe who are active participants in their relationship with God! The reason we are called "the bride" is because Jesus is in love with us, the way a groom loves a bride!

It's important to remember that people are not perfect, and therefore, neither is the church.

God's heart for His people isn't complicated. He loves us, and He wants us to encounter His love and realize its depths for us. This realization changes everything.

READ OUT LOUD: Ephesians 4:11-16

This passage explains how the church is to equip the saints. Take time to discuss this Scripture.

Isaiah 56:7

...my Temple will be called a house of prayer for all nations.

The Church (people of God) is called to be connected, glorifying Jesus, maturing in love, and functioning in unity as one body to make Jesus famous on the earth! We do this by showing the world the nature and character of God as well as by leading and influencing the world through the power of the Holy Spirit that lives in us!

Important roles of the Church:

- Ministers to the heart of God (tell Him and show Him we love Him)
- Hosts the manifest presence of God.
- Equips people with tools for life and spreads the Gospel.
- Provides a place where people can receive healing.
- Disciples the flock / family.
- Makes space for the people of God to create in His presence.
- Takes care of widows.
- Takes care of orphans.
- Takes care of the poor and needy.

The Church should be going out into all the world, making disciples. We bring the heart of God and the light of Jesus to dark places.

Take a moment to pray that the church finds the courage to rise up bold as a lion in these days to infiltrate places of influence in the world: the education system, government, the justice system, family, entertainment, media, the arts, and business.

The local church is what makes up the body of Christ. It's important to be part of a like-minded community of believers for encouragement and sharpening. It is vital to be connected to a local church with healthy, honest, relational leaders. The core beliefs of the church should mostly match yours, but you may be hard-pressed to find a church that shares all the same beliefs as you. Diversity is beautiful in the kingdom of God! It's important to value those in the church who have different beliefs from you. God loves us all to our very core, and people living according to their own personal convictions is biblical. It's not about being right — it's about being active participants in the family!

It's not what we do. It's who we are!

Song Suggestion: "The Church — Live" by Bethel Music

Lesson 7.2 | Grace Gifts

Ephesians 4:11

Now these are the gifts Christ gave to the church: the apostles, the prophets, the evangelists, and the pastors and teachers.

HOW EACH GIFT FUNCTIONS:

Apostle	Brings heaven to earth. A builder.
Prophet	Points the way. Brings God's heart. Has blueprints.
Evangelist	Fills up heaven.
Pastor	Protects and nurtures the flock.
Teacher	Dissects Scripture, culture, and context to discover and teach the truth

Note: It is not possible to function healthily in any of these gifts without the grace of God empowering you to do so. These require heavy lifting. You need Jesus!

READ OUT LOUD: Ephesians 4:12-16

You learn which one you are called to by looking at your natural bent. If you are attracted to miracles, you might be an apostle. If you are naturally protective and nurturing, you might be a pastor… and so on.

It's VITAL to know that these grace gifts are given to you without titles, positions, and paychecks. These are HEART postures designed to build up and strengthen the body of Christ! You may have a position or title, but it's who you are, not what you do. Therefore, you are gifted by God's grace to walk in this gift everywhere you go, no matter who is around. It's not just for Sunday morning service.

Maybe you're well-rounded and feel you could operate in any of these gifts. That could mean you are an apostle. A contractor who builds a home is ultimately responsible for the whole project. Plumbing, electrical, drywall… the contractor has to make sure all the details come together.

Dig into these grace gifts. They make a way for the church to be united, encouraged, perfected, equipped, and so much more. We need all of these operating in the church!

!!BEWARE!!:

- Don't let any of these gifts become an idol.
- Do not love the gift more than the One who gives the gift.
- Do not love the gifts in another more than you love the person.

Lesson 7.3 | Spiritual Gifts

1 Corinthians 12:7

A spiritual gift is given to each of us so we can help each other.

The purpose of spiritual gifts is to encourage, edify, and mature the body of Christ.

Remember: It's not what we do. It's who we are. The Church is not a building. The Church is a people!

Spiritual gifts help us as a body to operate and function as one. Stir up the gifts! Call out the gold you see in each other.

READ OUT LOUD: 1 Corinthians 12

This Scripture explains there are MANY spiritual gifts, and the author lists SOME of those gifts that the Spirit of God gives.

SOME SPIRITUAL GIFTS

Wisdom, knowledge, faith, healing, miracles, prophecy, the discerning of spirits, tongues, interpretation of tongues, leadership, service, teaching, giving, and mercy.

Spiritual gifts include things you do that seem accelerated because of God's hand on your life — things you do with excellence and without much effort that help the whole body of Christ.

DISCUSS WITH THE GROUP:

What spiritual gift(s) do you have?

Encourage one another in your gifts.

Lesson 7.4 | Leadership

Leadership is one of those topics that could be a 300-page book all by itself.

God, Jesus, and the Holy Spirit are the ONLY perfect leaders.

Here are some Scriptures that give us a wide lens view of biblical leadership.

1 Timothy 4:12

Don't let anyone think less of you because you are young. Be an example to all believers in what you say, in the way you live, in your love, your faith, and your purity.

Proverbs 11:14

Without wise leadership, a nation falls; there is safety in having many advisers.

READ OUT LOUD: Matthew 20:26-28

Philippians 2:3

Don't be selfish; don't try to impress others. Be humble, thinking of others as better than yourselves.

There are SO many Scriptures on this topic. Explore some others! Check out Hebrews, Galatians, 1 Peter, and 1 Thessalonians.

In a nutshell, ***good leaders lead like Jesus***. He had the identity and authority of a king, and yet He served the people like a servant. Jesus was never wondering what the people He served could do for him. He was always looking for ways to serve, grow, and love them.

By today's standards, Jesus wouldn't be very popular or successful. He traveled and ministered with the same people. He wasn't worried about being popular or relevant, so we probably wouldn't be inviting Him to speak at a youth conference. He was particularly concerned about seeing the people in front of him really well, especially those whom society didn't seem to care for.

How you define success should always have to do with encountering Jesus and transformed hearts. So, how do we do this?

Really seek to see people as Jesus does:

- Have authentic relationships with the people you lead
- Love them where they are.
- Give people the freedom to be themselves in your presence.
- Be approachable.
- Create a culture of feedback.

Leaders need to be really safe people.

One mistake leaders make these days is that they lead alone. Lonely leaders create tired leaders who are running on empty with nothing to give anyone. This is not the model Jesus gave.

8. MATURITY

Lesson 8.1 | Romans Part 1

Romans and Hebrews serve as the most meaty books of the whole Bible. Don't rush.

Romans 8:5-8

Those who are dominated by the sinful nature think about sinful things, but those who are controlled by the Holy Spirit think about things that please the Spirit. So letting your sinful nature control your mind leads to death. But letting the Spirit control your mind leads to life and peace. For the sinful nature is always hostile to God. It never did obey God's laws, and it never will. That's why those who are still under the control of their sinful nature can never please God.

SUGGESTION: Kings and queens don't hang out in the slums. Why? Because their identity/status demands a palace. We say things like "Kill your flesh" or "You need to die to yourself," and while these statements are true, the heart behind them is all wrong. These phrases communicate that we are scum! Jesus didn't die for scum. We are kings and queens. We are His children, and He loves us! Our behaviors (good and bad) are driven by the way we see ourselves. See yourself rightly. Your mind, will, and emotions will be singing a new tune when your identity is realized. Knowing your identity is KEY.

READ OUT LOUD & DISCUSS: Luke 8:4-15

2 Corinthians 13:11

Dear brothers and sisters, I close my letter with these last words: Be joyful. Grow to maturity. Encourage each other. Live in harmony and peace. Then the God of love and peace will be with you.

Take time to encourage one another. Point out someone's specific forward steps. Celebrate your friends who are indeed growing in Christ. Continue to be an encouragement to them.

Lesson 8.2 | Romans Part 2

<u>Romans 8:9-10</u>

But you are not controlled by your sinful nature. You are controlled by the Spirit if you have the Spirit of God living in you. (And remember that those who do not have the Spirit of Christ living in them do not belong to him at all.) And Christ lives within you, so even though your body will die because of sin, the Spirit gives you life because you have been made right with God.

The Spirit of Christ = Life / Essence of Jesus

In our lives today, we embody the qualities that Jesus demonstrated during His time on earth. Simply put, we do what He would have done.

We are the MOST alive when we live AWARE that the Spirit of Christ lives in us!

<u>Romans 8:11</u>

The Spirit of God, who raised Jesus from the dead, lives in you. And just as God raised Christ Jesus from the dead, he will give life to your mortal bodies by this same Spirit living within you.

Jesus gives you access to an abundant life NOW. There may be places in your heart that feel dead. Life happens, and pain changes the landscape of our hearts.

But the Spirit of the living God wants to bring everything dead back to life.

Journal about letting go of whatever seems dead in your heart. Maybe it's childlike faith. Maybe it's worship. Maybe it's a relationship that has broken your heart and needs to be surrendered to God.

Let go of everything holding you back from being one with Jesus.

REMEMBER**: He is clsoer than your skin, and He will not separate Himself from you.**

Lesson 8.3 | Love

Ephesians 4:15-17

Instead, we will speak the truth in love, growing in every way more and more like Christ, who is the head of his body, the church. He makes the whole body fit together perfectly. As each part does its own special work, it helps the other parts grow, so that the whole body is healthy and growing and full of love.

Christ is the head = Christ is the LEADER.

The whole body = the whole CHURCH.

(not just your local church, but the GLOBAL CHURCH)

Speak the truth in love

Strong connections and good relationships allow you more liberty to speak plainly. Make sure they know your heart before they know your criticism, correction, or negative feedback. If there's not a strong bond between two people, there's not a lot of liberty to speak boldly.

Maturity in this area is Leadership 101.

Love is a choice.

Loving your family. Loving a spouse. Loving friends. You are free to choose.

1 John 4:19

We love each other because he loved us first.

Think of love like a flow chart. Here's the flow:

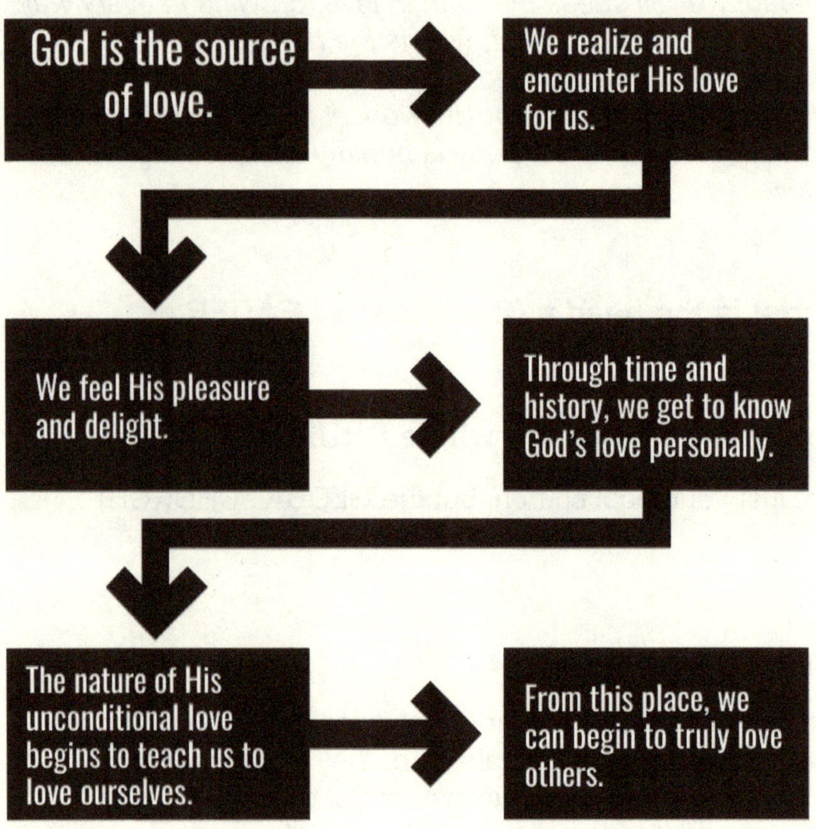

Lesson 8.4 | The Standard

Ephesians 4:13 NLT

This will continue until we all come to such unity in our faith and knowledge of God's Son that we will be mature in the Lord, measuring up to the full and complete standard of Christ.

THE STANDARD FOR OUR LIFE IS THE LIFE OF CHRIST.

Don't compare yourself to your friends, your family, strangers, or even your heroes.

Good role models may be those who have achieved a lot — those who are successful, well-spoken, athletic, have good morals, education, a good family, or wealth. It's not wrong to have those people in our lives that we want to follow or model; however, the standard is still Jesus.

Behavior is led by belief. What you believe in your heart will manifest in your behaviors.

Look at Jesus. Study what beliefs led Him to behave the way He did.

Look at different stories in the gospels. Look at His heart. See what His heart beats for. What is He passionate about? What does His passion look like? Discuss!

The standard is Jesus. His heart. His vision. His suffering. His death. His resurrection.

John 6:53

So Jesus said again, "I tell you the truth, unless you eat the flesh of the Son of Man and drink his blood, you cannot have eternal life within you."

Lesson 8.5 | Unity

Common misunderstandings:

- Everyone thinks the same.
- Everyone believes the same.
- Everyone agrees with no conflict.
- Everyone lays down their own conviction to go with someone else's conviction.

These are all examples of uniformity, and it's not what God wants.

There are two places to be in unity. Number 2 on the list will happen automatically if number 1 happens first:

1. Unity with God   2. Unity in the body of Christ

John 17:21

I pray that they will all be one, just as you and I are one—as you are in me, Father, and I am in you. And may they be in us so that the world will believe you sent me.

When you are one with God, you understand His heart, you have His vision for yourself, you can see others through the lens of Jesus, and all these things lead to deep love for the body of Christ.

Iron sharpening is not a soft or tender process. We are supposed to rub against each other!

Good leaders move toward disagreement. They are willing to engage in difficult conversations, have the relational and emotional intelligence to hold them correctly, and move hearts toward one another in love.

Unity comes when we listen to understand instead of listening to respond.

1 Corinthians 12:12-13

The human body has many parts, but these parts make up one whole body. So it is with the body of Christ. Some of us are Jews, some are Gentiles, some are slaves, and some are free. But we have all been baptized into one body by one Spirit, and we all share the same Spirit.

READ OUT LOUD: 1 Corinthians 12:24-26

Ephesians 4:16

He makes the whole body fit together perfectly. As each part does its own special work, it helps the other parts grow, so that the whole body is healthy and growing and full of love.

There are different denominations, expressions, personal preferences, generational preferences, languages, songs, Bible translations, and traditions. If Jesus is at the center, none of these differences will matter. We simply can't let our preference be the main thing.

Jesus is glorified when we are one with Him, worshipping in spirit and in truth. Jesus is glorified when we disagree really well. Jesus is glorified when we use the Jesus lens to see each other.

True unity is when Jesus is glorified in our lives.

We are the Church!

Lesson 8.6 | Maturity

Maturity is moving from being a recipient of grace to being responsible for extending it.

Being part of Kingdom solutions for the Earth's problems is our mandate.

<u>Mark 1:14-15</u>

Later on, after John was arrested, Jesus went into Galilee, where he preached God's Good News. "The time promised by God has come at last!" he announced. "The Kingdom of God is near! Repent of your sins and believe the Good News!"

In this Scripture, we see John taking responsibility and stewardship for the Kingdom of God that was inside of Him. John could have gone home and cried about his suffering. Instead, John knew everyone needed what had been given to him!

We teach what we know. We impart what we live.

You have a unique calling and unique passions. You have overcome hard things. The victory you live in is not only for you, but also for the community around you! Impart the freedom you have obtained. Your specific testimony is a prophetic declaration for God to do it again for someone else.

Hebrews 5:14

Solid food is for those who are mature, who, through training, have the skill to recognize the difference between right and wrong.

The other side to maturity is being able to handle the deep revelations that the Spirit is always inviting you into! Staying open-hearted and open-minded in order to grow beyond your current revelations requires a tension you will continually live in. Hold everything loosely and stay flexible as you grow in the Lord. Trust the Holy Spirit to lead you into all truth.

Lastly, not everyone will be ready for the revelations you have. It's important to discern (an inner knowing from the Lord) when to speak and when not to speak. Follow the leading of the Holy Spirit. Your leadership and obedience in this will be most helpful to you and everyone around you.

ENGAGE

Don't answer these questions quickly. Take some time and be challenged by answering them slowly.

What does it look like for you to represent Christ on the earth?

How does it work in your family?

How does it work at your job?

What does it look like at church?

What are some of your desires / dreams?

How can you disagree with people in a safe way?

How do you handle it when others are unsafe to disagree with?

What problems do you want to solve for the world?

What kind of people are your favorite?

Who do you want to be? (This is not, “What do you want to do?”)

GROUP DISCUSSION:

Explore some of your limiting beliefs and discuss with the group in vulnerability how you can practice a better thought process for your beliefs.

WHAT NOW?

You finished this book. Confetti!

Hopefully, you learned a lot and built strong relationships. Now, it's time to put it all into practice. I am praying you feel pregnant with the love of God, passion, purpose, and power.

Isaiah 60:1-3

Arise, Jerusalem! Let your light shine for all to see. For the glory of the Lord rises to shine on you. Darkness as black as night covers all the nations of the earth, but the glory of the Lord rises and appears over you. All nations will come to your light; mighty kings will come to see your radiance.

You don't have a light. You ARE a light. Shine bright out there!

Romans 8:19-23

For all creation is waiting eagerly for that future day when God will reveal who his children really are. Against its will, all creation was subjected to God's curse. But with eager hope, the creation looks forward to the day when it will join God's children in glorious freedom from death and decay. For we know that all creation has been groaning as in the pains of childbirth right up to the present time.

Creation is groaning for sons and daughters confident in their father's love, filled with the love of God, operating in authority and power. You're here to change the world.

The Shalom Collective is a resource for teenage girls and women from all walks. The invitation is to learn how to live from rest while growing roots in Jesus.

The Shalom Collective hosts events, zoom calls, themed retreats, and relational community meetings to connect the lonely and isolated.

Visit www.theshalomcollective.com for more information.

www.ingramcontent.com/pod-product-compliance
Lightning Source LLC
La Vergne TN
LVHW090613110826
845146LV00001B/367

* 9 7 9 8 9 9 3 6 7 5 4 1 1 *